Individual Studies for Grade 5

A Year of Lesson Plans
for Language Arts, Math, and Science

by
Sonya Shafer

Individual Studies for Grade 5: A Year of Lesson Plans for Language Arts, Math, and Science
© 2016, Sonya Shafer

Cover Design: John Shafer and Sarah Shafer

ISBN 978-1-61634-345-3 printed
ISBN 978-1-61634-346-0 electronic download

Published by
Simply Charlotte Mason, LLC
930 New Hope Road #11-892
Lawrenceville, Georgia 30045
simplycharlottemason.com

Printed by PrintLogic, Inc.
Monroe, Georgia, USA

Contents

How to Use

Most school subjects can be taught to your whole family together, but some subjects are best taught individually so you can progress at the student's pace. This book of lesson plans contains suggestions and assignments for individual work for students in grade 5. Complete one lesson plan per day to finish these studies in a school year.

The lesson plans in this book cover language arts, science, and math.

Language Arts

Students will begin a study of the parts of speech as well as continue to progress in spelling, capitalization, punctuation, and English usage guidelines using the literary passages presented in *Spelling Wisdom, Book 2*, and the guided discovery lessons in *Using Language Well, Book 2*. The first half of these books will be covered this year; the rest will be completed in grade 6.

Written narration will be assigned to encourage your student to continue to progress in capturing his thoughts on paper and applying guidelines he has learned about English usage and mechanics. Rubrics and further instructions are provided in the *Using Language Well, Book 2, Teacher Guide and Answer Key*.

Science

Science can be done individually, or if you have more than one student in grades 1–6, they may all do one science course together. Simply Charlotte Mason has several to choose from.

Nature Study is an important part of science studies; be sure to include it. Follow the Nature Study suggestions in your selected science course or use the nature notebook, *Journaling a Year in Nature*, to guide your weekly study. Nature Study can be done all together as a family, but we have included reminders in these individual plans too.

Math

Use the math curriculum of your choice. These lesson plans will include reminders to work on it. As with other individual work, be sure to go at your student's pace.

Complete Year's Resources List

- *Spelling Wisdom, Book 2*
  Students will complete the first half of this book this year; the rest will be covered in grade 6.
- *Using Language Well, Book 2, Student Book*
  Students will complete the first half of this book this year; the rest will be covered in grade 6.
- *Using Language Well, Book 2, Teacher Guide and Answer Key*
- Simply Charlotte Mason (SCM) science course of choice
- *Journaling a Year in Nature* notebooks, one per person (optional)
- Math course of choice
- Typing course of choice

Note: All resources except math and typing are available from Simply Charlotte Mason.

Term 1

(12 weeks; 5 lessons/week)

Term 1 Resources List
- *Spelling Wisdom, Book 2* ✓
- *Using Language Well, Book 2, Student Book* ✓
- *Using Language Well, Book 2, Teacher Guide and Answer Key* ✓
- Simply Charlotte Mason (SCM) science course of choice
- *Journaling a Year in Nature* notebooks (optional) ✓
- Typing course of choice ✓
- Math course of choice ✓

Weekly Schedule

Day One	Day Two	Day Three	Day Four	Day Five
Math (20–30 min.)	Math (20–30 min.)	Math (20–30 min.)	Math (20–30 min.)	Math (20–30 min.)
	Science (20–30 min.)		Science (20–30 min.)	(Nature Study)
Typing (10–15 min.)	Spelling Wisdom & Using Language Well (15–20 min.)	Typing (10–15 min.)		Spelling Wisdom & Using Language Well (15–20 min.)

Lesson 1

Materials Needed
- Math course of choice
- Typing course of choice

Math: Work on your selected math curriculum for about 30 minutes.

Typing: Work on your selected typing course for about 15 minutes.

Lesson 2

Materials Needed
- Math course of choice
- SCM science course of choice
- *Spelling Wisdom, Book 2*
- *Using Language Well, Book 2, Student Book*
- *Using Language Well, Book 2, Teacher Guide and Answer Key*

Math: Work on your selected math curriculum for about 30 minutes.

Science: In your SCM science course, complete the first assignment for Week 1.

Spelling and Grammar: Complete *Using Language Well, Book 2,* lesson 1.

Tip: The lessons assigned in Using Language Well, Book 2, *are designed to be completed independently. Check your student's work and oversee the dictation portion when he is ready. See the* Using Language Well, Book 2, Teacher Guide and Answer Key *for details.*

Lesson 3

Materials Needed
- Math course of choice
- Typing course of choice

Math: Work on your selected math curriculum for about 30 minutes.

Typing: Work on your selected typing course for about 15 minutes.

Lesson 4

Materials Needed
- SCM science course of choice
- Math course of choice

Science: In your SCM science course, complete the second assignment for Week 1.

Math: Work on your selected math curriculum for about 30 minutes.

Lesson 5

Materials Needed
- Math course of choice
- *Spelling Wisdom, Book 2*
- *Using Language Well, Book 2, Student Book*
- *Using Language Well, Book 2, Teacher Guide and Answer Key*
- *Journaling a Year in Nature* notebooks (optional)

Math: Work on your selected math curriculum for about 30 minutes.

Spelling and Grammar: Complete *Using Language Well, Book 2,* lesson 2.

Nature Study: Take the whole family outside for nature study.

Tip: Follow the Nature Study suggestions in your SCM science course or use the nature notebook, Journaling a Year in Nature, *to guide your weekly study.*

Lesson 6

Materials Needed
- Math course of choice
- Typing course of choice

Math: Work on your selected math curriculum for about 30 minutes.

Typing: Work on your selected typing course for about 15 minutes.

Reminder: Assign your student to write one narration from his history, geography, Bible, or science readings this week. Use Rubric 2.1 from Using Language Well, Book 2, Teacher Guide and Answer Key *to help you evaluate his writing. Continue oral narrations daily.*

Lesson 7

Materials Needed
- Math course of choice
- SCM science course of choice

- *Spelling Wisdom, Book 2*
- *Using Language Well, Book 2, Student Book*
- *Using Language Well, Book 2, Teacher Guide and Answer Key*

Math: Work on your selected math curriculum for about 30 minutes.

Science: In your SCM science course, complete the first assignment for Week 2.

Spelling and Grammar: Complete *Using Language Well, Book 2*, lesson 3.

Lesson 8

Materials Needed
- Math course of choice
- Typing course of choice

Math: Work on your selected math curriculum for about 30 minutes.

Typing: Work on your selected typing course for about 15 minutes.

Lesson 9

Materials Needed
- SCM science course of choice
- Math course of choice

Science: In your SCM science course, complete the second assignment for Week 2.

Math: Work on your selected math curriculum for about 30 minutes.

Lesson 10

Materials Needed
- Math course of choice
- *Spelling Wisdom, Book 2*
- *Using Language Well, Book 2, Student Book*
- *Using Language Well, Book 2, Teacher Guide and Answer Key*
- *Journaling a Year in Nature* notebooks (optional)

Math: Work on your selected math curriculum for about 30 minutes.

Spelling and Grammar: Complete *Using Language Well, Book 2*, lesson 4.

Nature Study: Take the whole family outside for nature study.

Tip: Follow the Nature Study suggestions in your SCM science course or use the nature notebook, Journaling a Year in Nature, *to guide your weekly study.*

Lesson 11

Materials Needed
- Math course of choice
- Typing course of choice

Math: Work on your selected math curriculum for about 30 minutes.

Typing: Work on your selected typing course for about 15 minutes.

Reminder: Assign your student to write one narration from his history, geography, Bible, or science readings this week. Use Rubric 2.1 from Using Language Well, Book 2, Teacher Guide and Answer Key *to help you evaluate his writing. Continue oral narrations daily.*

Lesson 12

Materials Needed
- Math course of choice
- SCM science course of choice
- *Spelling Wisdom, Book 2*
- *Using Language Well, Book 2, Student Book*
- *Using Language Well, Book 2, Teacher Guide and Answer Key*

Math: Work on your selected math curriculum for about 30 minutes.

Science: In your SCM science course, complete the first assignment for Week 3.

Spelling and Grammar: Complete *Using Language Well, Book 2,* lesson 5.

Lesson 13

Materials Needed
- Math course of choice
- Typing course of choice

Math: Work on your selected math curriculum for about 30 minutes.

Typing: Work on your selected typing course for about 15 minutes.

Tip: If your student would like to, encourage him to keep a Book of Mottoes, or a commonplace book,—a journal in which he records personally selected quotations, poetry, excerpts, or Scripture passages that are meaningful to him. You might allow him to purchase a special journal for this ongoing project. You will see periodic reminders in these lesson plans; mention them only if your student is interested.

Lesson 14

Materials Needed
- SCM science course of choice
- Math course of choice

Science: In your SCM science course, complete the second assignment for Week 3.

Math: Work on your selected math curriculum for about 30 minutes.

Lesson 15

Materials Needed
- Math course of choice
- *Spelling Wisdom, Book 2*
- *Using Language Well, Book 2, Student Book*
- *Using Language Well, Book 2, Teacher Guide and Answer Key*
- *Journaling a Year in Nature* notebooks (optional)

Math: Work on your selected math curriculum for about 30 minutes.

Spelling and Grammar: Complete Using Language Well, Book 2, lesson 6.

Nature Study: Take the whole family outside for nature study.

Tip: Follow the Nature Study suggestions in your SCM science course or use the nature notebook, Journaling a Year in Nature, *to guide your weekly study.*

Lesson 16

Materials Needed
- Math course of choice
- Typing course of choice

Math: Work on your selected math curriculum for about 30 minutes.

Typing: Work on your selected typing course for about 15 minutes.

Notes

> **Reminder:** *Assign your student to write one narration from his history, geography, Bible, or science readings this week. Use Rubric 2.1 from* Using Language Well, Book 2, Teacher Guide and Answer Key *to help you evaluate his writing. Continue oral narrations daily.*

Lesson 17

Materials Needed
- Math course of choice
- SCM science course of choice
- *Spelling Wisdom, Book 2*
- *Using Language Well, Book 2, Student Book*
- *Using Language Well, Book 2, Teacher Guide and Answer Key*

Math: Work on your selected math curriculum for about 30 minutes.

Science: In your SCM science course, complete the first assignment for Week 4.

Spelling and Grammar: Complete *Using Language Well, Book 2,* lesson 7.

Lesson 18

Materials Needed
- Math course of choice
- Typing course of choice

Math: Work on your selected math curriculum for about 30 minutes.

Typing: Work on your selected typing course for about 15 minutes.

Lesson 19

Materials Needed
- SCM science course of choice
- Math course of choice

Science: In your SCM science course, complete the second assignment for Week 4.

Math: Work on your selected math curriculum for about 30 minutes.

Lesson 20

Materials Needed
- Math course of choice
- *Spelling Wisdom, Book 2*

- *Using Language Well, Book 2, Student Book*
- *Using Language Well, Book 2, Teacher Guide and Answer Key*
- *Journaling a Year in Nature* notebooks (optional)

Math: Work on your selected math curriculum for about 30 minutes.

Spelling and Grammar: Complete *Using Language Well, Book 2,* lesson 8.

Nature Study: Take the whole family outside for nature study.

Lesson 21

Materials Needed
- Math course of choice
- Typing course of choice

Math: Work on your selected math curriculum for about 30 minutes.

Typing: Work on your selected typing course for about 15 minutes.

Reminder: Assign your student to write one narration from his history, geography, Bible, or science readings this week. Use Rubric 2.1 from Using Language Well, Book 2, Teacher Guide and Answer Key *to help you evaluate his writing. Continue oral narrations daily.*

Lesson 22

Materials Needed
- Math course of choice
- SCM science course of choice
- *Spelling Wisdom, Book 2*
- *Using Language Well, Book 2, Student Book*
- *Using Language Well, Book 2, Teacher Guide and Answer Key*

Math: Work on your selected math curriculum for about 30 minutes.

Science: In your SCM science course, complete the first assignment for Week 5.

Spelling and Grammar: Complete *Using Language Well, Book 2,* lesson 9.

Lesson 23

Materials Needed
- Math course of choice
- Typing course of choice

Math: Work on your selected math curriculum for about 30 minutes.

Typing: Work on your selected typing course for about 15 minutes.

Lesson 24

Materials Needed
- SCM science course of choice
- Math course of choice

Science: In your SCM science course, complete the second assignment for Week 5.

Math: Work on your selected math curriculum for about 30 minutes.

Lesson 25

Materials Needed
- Math course of choice
- *Spelling Wisdom, Book 2*
- *Using Language Well, Book 2, Student Book*
- *Using Language Well, Book 2, Teacher Guide and Answer Key*
- *Journaling a Year in Nature* notebooks (optional)

Math: Work on your selected math curriculum for about 30 minutes.

Spelling and Grammar: Complete *Using Language Well, Book 2,* lesson 10.

Nature Study: Take the whole family outside for nature study.

Lesson 26

Materials Needed
- Math course of choice
- Typing course of choice

Math: Work on your selected math curriculum for about 30 minutes.

Typing: Work on your selected typing course for about 15 minutes.

Reminder: Assign your student to write one narration from his history, geography, Bible, or science readings this week. Use Rubric 2.1 from Using Language Well, Book 2, Teacher Guide and Answer Key *to help you evaluate his writing. Continue oral narrations daily.*

Lesson 27

Materials Needed
- Math course of choice

- SCM science course of choice
- *Spelling Wisdom, Book 2*
- *Using Language Well, Book 2, Student Book*
- *Using Language Well, Book 2, Teacher Guide and Answer Key*

Math: Work on your selected math curriculum for about 30 minutes.

Science: In your SCM science course, complete the first assignment for Week 6.

Spelling and Grammar: Complete *Using Language Well, Book 2,* lesson 11.

Lesson 28

Materials Needed
- Math course of choice
- Typing course of choice

Math: Work on your selected math curriculum for about 30 minutes.

Typing: Work on your selected typing course for about 15 minutes.

Tip: Remind your student to record in his Book of Mottoes any meaningful quotations, poetry, excerpts, or Scripture passages from recent readings (if he is interested in that ongoing project).

Lesson 29

Materials Needed
- SCM science course of choice
- Math course of choice

Science: In your SCM science course, complete the second assignment for Week 6.

Math: Work on your selected math curriculum for about 30 minutes.

Lesson 30

Materials Needed
- Math course of choice
- *Spelling Wisdom, Book 2*
- *Using Language Well, Book 2, Student Book*
- *Using Language Well, Book 2, Teacher Guide and Answer Key*
- *Journaling a Year in Nature* notebooks (optional)

Math: Work on your selected math curriculum for about 30 minutes.

Spelling and Grammar: Complete *Using Language Well, Book 2,* lesson 12.

Nature Study: Take the whole family outside for nature study.

Lesson 31

Materials Needed
- Math course of choice
- Typing course of choice

Math: Work on your selected math curriculum for about 30 minutes.

Typing: Work on your selected typing course for about 15 minutes.

Reminder: Assign your student to write one narration from his history, geography, Bible, or science readings this week. Use Rubric 2.1 from Using Language Well, Book 2, Teacher Guide and Answer Key *to help you evaluate his writing. Continue oral narrations daily.*

Lesson 32

Materials Needed
- Math course of choice
- SCM science course of choice
- *Spelling Wisdom, Book 2*
- *Using Language Well, Book 2, Student Book*
- *Using Language Well, Book 2, Teacher Guide and Answer Key*

Math: Work on your selected math curriculum for about 30 minutes.

Science: In your SCM science course, complete the first assignment for Week 7.

Spelling and Grammar: Complete *Using Language Well, Book 2,* lesson 13.

Lesson 33

Materials Needed
- Math course of choice
- Typing course of choice

Math: Work on your selected math curriculum for about 30 minutes.

Typing: Work on your selected typing course for about 15 minutes.

Lesson 34

Materials Needed
- SCM science course of choice
- Math course of choice

Science: In your SCM science course, complete the second assignment for Week 7.

Math: Work on your selected math curriculum for about 30 minutes.

Lesson 35

Materials Needed
- Math course of choice
- *Spelling Wisdom, Book 2*
- *Using Language Well, Book 2, Student Book*
- *Using Language Well, Book 2, Teacher Guide and Answer Key*
- *Journaling a Year in Nature* notebooks (optional)

Math: Work on your selected math curriculum for about 30 minutes.

Spelling and Grammar: Complete *Using Language Well, Book 2,* lesson 14.

Nature Study: Take the whole family outside for nature study.

Lesson 36

Materials Needed
- Math course of choice
- Typing course of choice

Math: Work on your selected math curriculum for about 30 minutes.

Typing: Work on your selected typing course for about 15 minutes.

Lesson 37

Materials Needed
- Math course of choice
- SCM science course of choice
- *Spelling Wisdom, Book 2*
- *Using Language Well, Book 2, Student Book*
- *Using Language Well, Book 2, Teacher Guide and Answer Key*

Math: Work on your selected math curriculum for about 30 minutes.

Science: In your SCM science course, complete the first assignment for Week 8.

Spelling and Grammar: Complete *Using Language Well, Book 2,* lesson 15.

Reminder: Assign your student to write one narration from his history, geography, Bible, or science readings this week. Use Rubric 2.2 from Using Language Well, Book 2, Teacher Guide and Answer Key *to help you evaluate his writing. Continue oral narrations daily.*

Lesson 38

Materials Needed
- Math course of choice
- Typing course of choice

Math: Work on your selected math curriculum for about 30 minutes.

Typing: Work on your selected typing course for about 15 minutes.

Lesson 39

Materials Needed
- SCM science course of choice
- Math course of choice

Science: In your SCM science course, complete the second assignment for Week 8.

Math: Work on your selected math curriculum for about 30 minutes.

Lesson 40

Materials Needed
- Math course of choice
- *Spelling Wisdom, Book 2*
- *Using Language Well, Book 2, Student Book*
- *Using Language Well, Book 2, Teacher Guide and Answer Key*
- *Journaling a Year in Nature* notebooks (optional)

Math: Work on your selected math curriculum for about 30 minutes.

Spelling and Grammar: Complete *Using Language Well, Book 2,* lesson 16.

Nature Study: Take the whole family outside for nature study.

Lesson 41

Materials Needed
- Math course of choice

- Typing course of choice

Math: Work on your selected math curriculum for about 30 minutes.

Typing: Work on your selected typing course for about 15 minutes.

Reminder: Assign your student to write one narration from his history, geography, Bible, or science readings this week. Use Rubric 2.2 from Using Language Well, Book 2, Teacher Guide and Answer Key *to help you evaluate his writing. Continue oral narrations daily.*

Lesson 42

Materials Needed
- Math course of choice
- SCM science course of choice
- *Spelling Wisdom, Book 2*
- *Using Language Well, Book 2, Student Book*
- *Using Language Well, Book 2, Teacher Guide and Answer Key*

Math: Work on your selected math curriculum for about 30 minutes.

Science: In your SCM science course, complete the first assignment for Week 9.

Spelling and Grammar: Complete *Using Language Well, Book 2,* lesson 17.

Lesson 43

Materials Needed
- Math course of choice
- Typing course of choice

Math: Work on your selected math curriculum for about 30 minutes.

Typing: Work on your selected typing course for about 15 minutes.

Tip: Remind your student to record in his Book of Mottoes any meaningful quotations, poetry, excerpts, or Scripture passages from recent readings (if he is interested in that ongoing project).

Lesson 44

Materials Needed
- SCM science course of choice
- Math course of choice

Notes

Science: In your SCM science course, complete the second assignment for Week 9.

Math: Work on your selected math curriculum for about 30 minutes.

Lesson 45

Materials Needed
- Math course of choice
- *Spelling Wisdom, Book 2*
- *Using Language Well, Book 2, Student Book*
- *Using Language Well, Book 2, Teacher Guide and Answer Key*
- *Journaling a Year in Nature* notebooks (optional)

Math: Work on your selected math curriculum for about 30 minutes.

Spelling and Grammar: Complete *Using Language Well, Book 2,* lesson 18.

Nature Study: Take the whole family outside for nature study.

Lesson 46

Materials Needed
- Math course of choice
- Typing course of choice

Math: Work on your selected math curriculum for about 30 minutes.

Typing: Work on your selected typing course for about 15 minutes.

Reminder: Assign your student to write one narration from his history, geography, Bible, or science readings this week. Use Rubric 2.2 from Using Language Well, Book 2, Teacher Guide and Answer Key *to help you evaluate his writing. Continue oral narrations daily.*

Lesson 47

Materials Needed
- Math course of choice
- SCM science course of choice
- *Spelling Wisdom, Book 2*
- *Using Language Well, Book 2, Student Book*
- *Using Language Well, Book 2, Teacher Guide and Answer Key*

Math: Work on your selected math curriculum for about 30 minutes.

Science: In your SCM science course, complete the first assignment for Week 10.

Spelling and Grammar: Complete *Using Language Well, Book 2,* lesson 19.

Lesson 48

Materials Needed
- Math course of choice
- Typing course of choice

Math: Work on your selected math curriculum for about 30 minutes.

Typing: Work on your selected typing course for about 15 minutes.

Lesson 49

Materials Needed
- SCM science course of choice
- Math course of choice

Science: In your SCM science course, complete the second assignment for Week 10.

Math: Work on your selected math curriculum for about 30 minutes.

Lesson 50

Materials Needed
- Math course of choice
- *Spelling Wisdom, Book 2*
- *Using Language Well, Book 2, Student Book*
- *Using Language Well, Book 2, Teacher Guide and Answer Key*
- *Journaling a Year in Nature* notebooks (optional)

Math: Work on your selected math curriculum for about 30 minutes.

Spelling and Grammar: Complete *Using Language Well, Book 2,* lesson 20.

Nature Study: Take the whole family outside for nature study.

Lesson 51

Materials Needed
- Math course of choice
- Typing course of choice

Math: Work on your selected math curriculum for about 30 minutes.

Typing: Work on your selected typing course for about 15 minutes.

Reminder: Assign your student to write one narration from his history, geography, Bible, or science readings this week. Use Rubric 2.2 from Using Language Well, Book 2, Teacher Guide and Answer Key *to help you evaluate his writing. Continue oral narrations daily.*

Lesson 52

Materials Needed
- Math course of choice
- SCM science course of choice
- *Spelling Wisdom, Book 2*
- *Using Language Well, Book 2, Student Book*
- *Using Language Well, Book 2, Teacher Guide and Answer Key*

Math: Work on your selected math curriculum for about 30 minutes.

Science: In your SCM science course, complete the first assignment for Week 11.

Spelling and Grammar: Complete *Using Language Well, Book 2,* lesson 21.

Lesson 53

Materials Needed
- Math course of choice
- Typing course of choice

Math: Work on your selected math curriculum for about 30 minutes.

Typing: Work on your selected typing course for about 15 minutes.

Lesson 54

Materials Needed
- SCM science course of choice
- Math course of choice

Science: In your SCM science course, complete the second assignment for Week 11.

Math: Work on your selected math curriculum for about 30 minutes.

Lesson 55

Materials Needed
- Math course of choice

- *Spelling Wisdom, Book 2*
- *Using Language Well, Book 2, Student Book*
- *Using Language Well, Book 2, Teacher Guide and Answer Key*
- *Journaling a Year in Nature* notebooks (optional)

Math: Work on your selected math curriculum for about 30 minutes.

Spelling and Grammar: Complete *Using Language Well, Book 2,* lesson 22.

Nature Study: Take the whole family outside for nature study.

Lesson 56

Materials Needed
- Math course of choice
- Typing course of choice

Math: Work on your selected math curriculum for about 30 minutes.

Typing: Work on your selected typing course for about 15 minutes.

Reminder: Assign your student to write one narration from his history, geography, Bible, or science readings this week. Use Rubric 2.2 from Using Language Well, Book 2, Teacher Guide and Answer Key *to help you evaluate his writing. Continue oral narrations daily.*

Lesson 57

Materials Needed
- Math course of choice
- SCM science course of choice
- *Spelling Wisdom, Book 2*
- *Using Language Well, Book 2, Student Book*
- *Using Language Well, Book 2, Teacher Guide and Answer Key*

Math: Work on your selected math curriculum for about 30 minutes.

Science: In your SCM science course, complete the first assignment for Week 12.

Spelling and Grammar: Complete *Using Language Well, Book 2,* lesson 23.

Lesson 58

Materials Needed
- Math course of choice
- Typing course of choice

Math: Work on your selected math curriculum for about 30 minutes.

Typing: Work on your selected typing course for about 15 minutes.

Tip: Remind your student to record in his Book of Mottoes any meaningful quotations, poetry, excerpts, or Scripture passages from recent readings (if he is interested in that ongoing project).

Lesson 59

Materials Needed
- SCM science course of choice
- Math course of choice

Science: In your SCM science course, complete the second assignment for Week 12.

Math: Work on your selected math curriculum for about 30 minutes.

Lesson 60

Materials Needed
- Math course of choice
- *Spelling Wisdom, Book 2*
- *Using Language Well, Book 2, Student Book*
- *Using Language Well, Book 2, Teacher Guide and Answer Key*
- *Journaling a Year in Nature* notebooks (optional)

Math: Work on your selected math curriculum for about 30 minutes.

Spelling and Grammar: Complete *Using Language Well, Book 2,* lesson 24.

Nature Study: Take the whole family outside for nature study.

Term 2

(12 weeks; 5 lessons/week)

Term 2 Resources List

- *Spelling Wisdom, Book 2*
- *Using Language Well, Book 2, Student Book*
- *Using Language Well, Book 2, Teacher Guide and Answer Key*
- Simply Charlotte Mason (SCM) science course of choice
- *Journaling a Year in Nature* notebooks (optional)
- Typing course of choice
- Math course of choice

Weekly Schedule

Day One	Day Two	Day Three	Day Four	Day Five
Math (20–30 min.)	Math (20–30 min.)	Math (20–30 min.)	Math (20–30 min.)	Math (20–30 min.)
(Nature Study)		Science (20–30 min.)		Science (20–30 min.)
Spelling Wisdom & Using Language Well (15–20 min.)	Typing (10–15 min.)	Spelling Wisdom & Using Language Well (15–20 min.)	Typing (10–15 min.)	

Lesson 61

Materials Needed
- Math course of choice
- *Spelling Wisdom, Book 2*
- *Using Language Well, Book 2, Student Book*
- *Using Language Well, Book 2, Teacher Guide and Answer Key*
- *Journaling a Year in Nature* notebooks (optional)

Math: Work on your selected math curriculum for about 30 minutes.

Spelling and Grammar: Complete *Using Language Well, Book 2,* lesson 25.

Nature Study: Take the whole family outside for nature study.

Reminder: Assign your student to write one narration from his history, geography, Bible, or science readings this week. Use Rubric 2.2 from Using Language Well, Book 2, Teacher Guide and Answer Key *to help you evaluate his writing. Continue oral narrations daily.*

Lesson 62

Materials Needed
- Math course of choice
- Typing course of choice

Math: Work on your selected math curriculum for about 30 minutes.

Typing: Work on your selected typing course for about 15 minutes.

Lesson 63

Materials Needed
- SCM science course of choice
- Math course of choice
- *Spelling Wisdom, Book 2*
- *Using Language Well, Book 2, Student Book*
- *Using Language Well, Book 2, Teacher Guide and Answer Key*

Science: In your SCM science course, complete the first assignment for Week 13.

Math: Work on your selected math curriculum for about 30 minutes.

Spelling and Grammar: Complete *Using Language Well, Book 2,* lesson 26.

Lesson 64

Materials Needed
- Math course of choice
- Typing course of choice

Math: Work on your selected math curriculum for about 30 minutes.

Typing: Work on your selected typing course for about 15 minutes.

Lesson 65

Materials Needed
- SCM science course of choice
- Math course of choice

Science: In your SCM science course, complete the second assignment for Week 13.

Math: Work on your selected math curriculum for about 30 minutes.

Lesson 66

Materials Needed
- Math course of choice
- *Spelling Wisdom, Book 2*
- *Using Language Well, Book 2, Student Book*
- *Using Language Well, Book 2, Teacher Guide and Answer Key*
- *Journaling a Year in Nature* notebooks (optional)

Math: Work on your selected math curriculum for about 30 minutes.

Spelling and Grammar: Complete *Using Language Well, Book 2,* lesson 27.

Nature Study: Take the whole family outside for nature study.

Reminder: Assign your student to write one narration from his history, geography, Bible, or science readings this week. Use Rubric 2.2 from Using Language Well, Book 2, Teacher Guide and Answer Key *to help you evaluate his writing. Continue oral narrations daily.*

Lesson 67

Materials Needed
- Math course of choice
- Typing course of choice

Math: Work on your selected math curriculum for about 30 minutes.

Typing: Work on your selected typing course for about 15 minutes.

Lesson 68

Materials Needed
- SCM science course of choice
- Math course of choice
- *Spelling Wisdom, Book 2*
- *Using Language Well, Book 2, Student Book*
- *Using Language Well, Book 2, Teacher Guide and Answer Key*

Science: In your SCM science course, complete the first assignment for Week 14.

Math: Work on your selected math curriculum for about 30 minutes.

Spelling and Grammar: Complete *Using Language Well, Book 2,* lesson 28.

Lesson 69

Materials Needed
- Math course of choice
- Typing course of choice

Math: Work on your selected math curriculum for about 30 minutes.

Typing: Work on your selected typing course for about 15 minutes.

Lesson 70

Materials Needed
- SCM science course of choice
- Math course of choice

Science: In your SCM science course, complete the second assignment for Week 14.

Math: Work on your selected math curriculum for about 30 minutes.

Lesson 71

Materials Needed
- Math course of choice
- *Spelling Wisdom, Book 2*
- *Using Language Well, Book 2, Student Book*
- *Using Language Well, Book 2, Teacher Guide and Answer Key*

- *Journaling a Year in Nature* notebooks (optional)

Math: Work on your selected math curriculum for about 30 minutes.

Spelling and Grammar: Complete *Using Language Well, Book 2,* lesson 29.

Nature Study: Take the whole family outside for nature study.

Reminder: Assign your student to write one narration from his history, geography, Bible, or science readings this week. Use Rubric 2.2 from Using Language Well, Book 2, Teacher Guide and Answer Key *to help you evaluate his writing. Continue oral narrations daily.*

Lesson 72

Materials Needed
- Math course of choice
- Typing course of choice

Math: Work on your selected math curriculum for about 30 minutes.

Typing: Work on your selected typing course for about 15 minutes.

Lesson 73

Materials Needed
- SCM science course of choice
- Math course of choice
- *Spelling Wisdom, Book 2*
- *Using Language Well, Book 2, Student Book*
- *Using Language Well, Book 2, Teacher Guide and Answer Key*

Science: In your SCM science course, complete the first assignment for Week 15.

Math: Work on your selected math curriculum for about 30 minutes.

Spelling and Grammar: Complete *Using Language Well, Book 2,* lesson 30.

Lesson 74

Materials Needed
- Math course of choice
- Typing course of choice

Math: Work on your selected math curriculum for about 30 minutes.

Typing: Work on your selected typing course for about 15 minutes.

Lesson 75

Materials Needed
- SCM science course of choice
- Math course of choice

Science: In your SCM science course, complete the second assignment for Week 15.

Math: Work on your selected math curriculum for about 30 minutes.

Tip: Remind your student to record in his Book of Mottoes any meaningful quotations, poetry, excerpts, or Scripture passages from recent readings (if he is interested in that ongoing project).

Lesson 76

Materials Needed
- Math course of choice
- *Spelling Wisdom, Book 2*
- *Using Language Well, Book 2, Student Book*
- *Using Language Well, Book 2, Teacher Guide and Answer Key*
- *Journaling a Year in Nature* notebooks (optional)

Math: Work on your selected math curriculum for about 30 minutes.

Spelling and Grammar: Complete *Using Language Well, Book 2,* lesson 31.

Nature Study: Take the whole family outside for nature study.

Reminder: Assign your student to write one narration from his history, geography, Bible, or science readings this week. Use Rubric 2.2 from Using Language Well, Book 2, Teacher Guide and Answer Key *to help you evaluate his writing. Continue oral narrations daily.*

Lesson 77

Materials Needed
- Math course of choice
- Typing course of choice

Math: Work on your selected math curriculum for about 30 minutes.

Typing: Work on your selected typing course for about 15 minutes.

Lesson 78

Materials Needed
- SCM science course of choice
- Math course of choice
- *Spelling Wisdom, Book 2*
- *Using Language Well, Book 2, Student Book*
- *Using Language Well, Book 2, Teacher Guide and Answer Key*

Science: In your SCM science course, complete the first assignment for Week 16.

Math: Work on your selected math curriculum for about 30 minutes.

Spelling and Grammar: Complete *Using Language Well, Book 2,* lesson 32.

Lesson 79

Materials Needed
- Math course of choice
- Typing course of choice

Math: Work on your selected math curriculum for about 30 minutes.

Typing: Work on your selected typing course for about 15 minutes.

Lesson 80

Materials Needed
- SCM science course of choice
- Math course of choice

Science: In your SCM science course, complete the second assignment for Week 16.

Math: Work on your selected math curriculum for about 30 minutes.

Lesson 81

Materials Needed
- Math course of choice
- *Spelling Wisdom, Book 2*
- *Using Language Well, Book 2, Student Book*
- *Using Language Well, Book 2, Teacher Guide and Answer Key*
- *Journaling a Year in Nature* notebooks (optional)

Math: Work on your selected math curriculum for about 30 minutes.

Spelling and Grammar: Complete *Using Language Well, Book 2,* lesson 33.

Nature Study: Take the whole family outside for nature study.

Reminder: Assign your student to write one narration from his history, geography, Bible, or science readings this week. Use Rubric 2.3 from Using Language Well, Book 2, Teacher Guide and Answer Key *to help you evaluate his writing. Continue oral narrations daily.*

Lesson 82

Materials Needed
- Math course of choice
- Typing course of choice

Math: Work on your selected math curriculum for about 30 minutes.

Typing: Work on your selected typing course for about 15 minutes.

Lesson 83

Materials Needed
- SCM science course of choice
- Math course of choice
- *Spelling Wisdom, Book 2*
- *Using Language Well, Book 2, Student Book*
- *Using Language Well, Book 2, Teacher Guide and Answer Key*

Science: In your SCM science course, complete the first assignment for Week 17.

Math: Work on your selected math curriculum for about 30 minutes.

Spelling and Grammar: Complete *Using Language Well, Book 2,* lesson 34.

Lesson 84

Materials Needed
- Math course of choice
- Typing course of choice

Math: Work on your selected math curriculum for about 30 minutes.

Typing: Work on your selected typing course for about 15 minutes.

Notes

Lesson 85

Materials Needed
- SCM science course of choice
- Math course of choice

Science: In your SCM science course, complete the second assignment for Week 17.

Math: Work on your selected math curriculum for about 30 minutes.

Lesson 86

Materials Needed
- Math course of choice
- *Spelling Wisdom, Book 2*
- *Using Language Well, Book 2, Student Book*
- *Using Language Well, Book 2, Teacher Guide and Answer Key*
- *Journaling a Year in Nature* notebooks (optional)

Math: Work on your selected math curriculum for about 30 minutes.

Spelling and Grammar: Complete *Using Language Well, Book 2,* lesson 35.

Nature Study: Take the whole family outside for nature study.

Reminder: Assign your student to write one narration from his history, geography, Bible, or science readings this week. Use Rubric 2.3 from Using Language Well, Book 2, Teacher Guide and Answer Key *to help you evaluate his writing. Continue oral narrations daily.*

Lesson 87

Materials Needed
- Math course of choice
- Typing course of choice

Math: Work on your selected math curriculum for about 30 minutes.

Typing: Work on your selected typing course for about 15 minutes.

Lesson 88

Materials Needed
- SCM science course of choice
- Math course of choice

- *Spelling Wisdom, Book 2*
- *Using Language Well, Book 2, Student Book*
- *Using Language Well, Book 2, Teacher Guide and Answer Key*

Science: In your SCM science course, complete the first assignment for Week 18.

Math: Work on your selected math curriculum for about 30 minutes.

Spelling and Grammar: Complete *Using Language Well, Book 2*, lesson 36.

Lesson 89

Materials Needed
- Math course of choice
- Typing course of choice

Math: Work on your selected math curriculum for about 30 minutes.

Typing: Work on your selected typing course for about 15 minutes.

Lesson 90

Materials Needed
- SCM science course of choice
- Math course of choice

Science: In your SCM science course, complete the second assignment for Week 18.

Math: Work on your selected math curriculum for about 30 minutes.

Tip: Remind your student to record in his Book of Mottoes any meaningful quotations, poetry, excerpts, or Scripture passages from recent readings (if he is interested in that ongoing project).

Lesson 91

Materials Needed
- Math course of choice
- *Spelling Wisdom, Book 2*
- *Using Language Well, Book 2, Student Book*
- *Using Language Well, Book 2, Teacher Guide and Answer Key*
- *Journaling a Year in Nature* notebooks (optional)

Math: Work on your selected math curriculum for about 30 minutes.

Notes

Spelling and Grammar: Complete *Using Language Well, Book 2,* lesson 37.

Nature Study: Take the whole family outside for nature study.

Reminder: Assign your student to write one narration from his history, geography, Bible, or science readings this week. Use Rubric 2.3 from Using Language Well, Book 2, Teacher Guide and Answer Key *to help you evaluate his writing. Continue oral narrations daily.*

Lesson 92

Materials Needed
- Math course of choice
- Typing course of choice

Math: Work on your selected math curriculum for about 30 minutes.

Typing: Work on your selected typing course for about 15 minutes.

Lesson 93

Materials Needed
- SCM science course of choice
- Math course of choice
- *Spelling Wisdom, Book 2*
- *Using Language Well, Book 2, Student Book*
- *Using Language Well, Book 2, Teacher Guide and Answer Key*

Science: In your SCM science course, complete the first assignment for Week 19.

Math: Work on your selected math curriculum for about 30 minutes.

Spelling and Grammar: Complete *Using Language Well, Book 2,* lesson 38.

Lesson 94

Materials Needed
- Math course of choice
- Typing course of choice

Math: Work on your selected math curriculum for about 30 minutes.

Typing: Work on your selected typing course for about 15 minutes.

Lesson 95

Materials Needed
- SCM science course of choice
- Math course of choice

Science: In your SCM science course, complete the second assignment for Week 19.

Math: Work on your selected math curriculum for about 30 minutes.

Lesson 96

Materials Needed
- Math course of choice
- *Spelling Wisdom, Book 2*
- *Using Language Well, Book 2, Student Book*
- *Using Language Well, Book 2, Teacher Guide and Answer Key*
- *Journaling a Year in Nature* notebooks (optional)

Math: Work on your selected math curriculum for about 30 minutes.

Spelling and Grammar: Complete *Using Language Well, Book 2,* lesson 39.

Nature Study: Take the whole family outside for nature study.

Reminder: Assign your student to write one narration from his history, geography, Bible, or science readings this week. Use Rubric 2.3 from Using Language Well, Book 2, Teacher Guide and Answer Key *to help you evaluate his writing. Continue oral narrations daily.*

Lesson 97

Materials Needed
- Math course of choice
- Typing course of choice

Math: Work on your selected math curriculum for about 30 minutes.

Typing: Work on your selected typing course for about 15 minutes.

Lesson 98

Materials Needed
- SCM science course of choice
- Math course of choice

Notes

- *Spelling Wisdom, Book 2*
- *Using Language Well, Book 2, Student Book*
- *Using Language Well, Book 2, Teacher Guide and Answer Key*

Science: In your SCM science course, complete the first assignment for Week 20.

Math: Work on your selected math curriculum for about 30 minutes.

Spelling and Grammar: Complete *Using Language Well, Book 2,* lesson 40.

Lesson 99

Materials Needed
- Math course of choice
- Typing course of choice

Math: Work on your selected math curriculum for about 30 minutes.

Typing: Work on your selected typing course for about 15 minutes.

Lesson 100

Materials Needed
- SCM science course of choice
- Math course of choice

Science: In your SCM science course, complete the second assignment for Week 20.

Math: Work on your selected math curriculum for about 30 minutes.

Lesson 101

Materials Needed
- Math course of choice
- *Spelling Wisdom, Book 2*
- *Using Language Well, Book 2, Student Book*
- *Using Language Well, Book 2, Teacher Guide and Answer Key*
- *Journaling a Year in Nature* notebooks (optional)

Math: Work on your selected math curriculum for about 30 minutes.

Spelling and Grammar: Complete *Using Language Well, Book 2,* lesson 41.

Nature Study: Take the whole family outside for nature study.

Reminder: Assign your student to write one narration from his history, geography, Bible, or science readings this week. Use Rubric 2.3 from Using Language Well, Book 2, Teacher Guide and Answer Key *to help you evaluate his writing. Continue oral narrations daily.*

Lesson 102

Materials Needed
- Math course of choice
- Typing course of choice

Math: Work on your selected math curriculum for about 30 minutes.

Typing: Work on your selected typing course for about 15 minutes.

Lesson 103

Materials Needed
- SCM science course of choice
- Math course of choice
- *Spelling Wisdom, Book 2*
- *Using Language Well, Book 2, Student Book*
- *Using Language Well, Book 2, Teacher Guide and Answer Key*

Science: In your SCM science course, complete the first assignment for Week 21.

Math: Work on your selected math curriculum for about 30 minutes.

Spelling and Grammar: Complete *Using Language Well, Book 2*, lesson 42.

Lesson 104

Materials Needed
- Math course of choice
- Typing course of choice

Math: Work on your selected math curriculum for about 30 minutes.

Typing: Work on your selected typing course for about 15 minutes.

Lesson 105

Materials Needed
- SCM science course of choice
- Math course of choice

Notes

Science: In your SCM science course, complete the second assignment for Week 21.

Math: Work on your selected math curriculum for about 30 minutes.

Lesson 106

Materials Needed
- Math course of choice
- *Spelling Wisdom, Book 2*
- *Using Language Well, Book 2, Student Book*
- *Using Language Well, Book 2, Teacher Guide and Answer Key*
- *Journaling a Year in Nature* notebooks (optional)

Math: Work on your selected math curriculum for about 30 minutes.

Spelling and Grammar: Complete *Using Language Well, Book 2,* lesson 43.

Nature Study: Take the whole family outside for nature study.

Reminder: Assign your student to write one narration from his history, geography, Bible, or science readings this week. Use Rubric 2.3 from Using Language Well, Book 2, Teacher Guide and Answer Key *to help you evaluate his writing. Continue oral narrations daily.*

Lesson 107

Materials Needed
- Math course of choice
- Typing course of choice

Math: Work on your selected math curriculum for about 30 minutes.

Typing: Work on your selected typing course for about 15 minutes.

Lesson 108

Materials Needed
- SCM science course of choice
- Math course of choice
- *Spelling Wisdom, Book 2*
- *Using Language Well, Book 2, Student Book*
- *Using Language Well, Book 2, Teacher Guide and Answer Key*

Science: In your SCM science course, complete the first assignment for Week 22.

Math: Work on your selected math curriculum for about 30 minutes.

Spelling and Grammar: Complete *Using Language Well, Book 2,* lesson 44.

Lesson 109

Materials Needed
- Math course of choice
- Typing course of choice

Math: Work on your selected math curriculum for about 30 minutes.

Typing: Work on your selected typing course for about 15 minutes.

Lesson 110

Materials Needed
- SCM science course of choice
- Math course of choice

Science: In your SCM science course, complete the second assignment for Week 22.

Math: Work on your selected math curriculum for about 30 minutes.

Lesson 111

Materials Needed
- Math course of choice
- *Spelling Wisdom, Book 2*
- *Using Language Well, Book 2, Student Book*
- *Using Language Well, Book 2, Teacher Guide and Answer Key*
- *Journaling a Year in Nature* notebooks (optional)

Math: Work on your selected math curriculum for about 30 minutes.

Spelling and Grammar: Complete *Using Language Well, Book 2,* lesson 45.

Nature Study: Take the whole family outside for nature study.

Reminder: Assign your student to write one narration from his history, geography, Bible, or science readings this week. Use Rubric 2.3 from Using Language Well, Book 2, Teacher Guide and Answer Key *to help you evaluate his writing. Continue oral narrations daily.*

Lesson 112

Materials Needed
- Math course of choice
- Typing course of choice

Math: Work on your selected math curriculum for about 30 minutes.

Typing: Work on your selected typing course for about 15 minutes.

Lesson 113

Materials Needed
- SCM science course of choice
- Math course of choice
- *Spelling Wisdom, Book 2*
- *Using Language Well, Book 2, Student Book*
- *Using Language Well, Book 2, Teacher Guide and Answer Key*

Science: In your SCM science course, complete the first assignment for Week 23.

Math: Work on your selected math curriculum for about 30 minutes.

Spelling and Grammar: Complete *Using Language Well, Book 2,* lesson 46.

Lesson 114

Materials Needed
- Math course of choice
- Typing course of choice

Math: Work on your selected math curriculum for about 30 minutes.

Typing: Work on your selected typing course for about 15 minutes.

Lesson 115

Materials Needed
- SCM science course of choice
- Math course of choice

Science: In your SCM science course, complete the second assignment for Week 23.

Math: Work on your selected math curriculum for about 30 minutes.

Lesson 116

Materials Needed
- Math course of choice
- *Spelling Wisdom, Book 2*
- *Using Language Well, Book 2, Student Book*
- *Using Language Well, Book 2, Teacher Guide and Answer Key*
- *Journaling a Year in Nature* notebooks (optional)

Math: Work on your selected math curriculum for about 30 minutes.

Spelling and Grammar: Complete *Using Language Well, Book 2*, lesson 47.

Nature Study: Take the whole family outside for nature study.

Reminder: Assign your student to write one narration from his history, geography, Bible, or science readings this week. Use Rubric 2.3 from Using Language Well, Book 2, Teacher Guide and Answer Key *to help you evaluate his writing. Continue oral narrations daily.*

Lesson 117

Materials Needed
- Math course of choice
- Typing course of choice

Math: Work on your selected math curriculum for about 30 minutes.

Typing: Work on your selected typing course for about 15 minutes.

Lesson 118

Materials Needed
- SCM science course of choice
- Math course of choice
- *Spelling Wisdom, Book 2*
- *Using Language Well, Book 2, Student Book*
- *Using Language Well, Book 2, Teacher Guide and Answer Key*

Science: In your SCM science course, complete the first assignment for Week 24.

Math: Work on your selected math curriculum for about 30 minutes.

Spelling and Grammar: Complete *Using Language Well, Book 2*, lesson 48.

Lesson 119

Materials Needed
- Math course of choice
- Typing course of choice

Math: Work on your selected math curriculum for about 30 minutes.

Typing: Work on your selected typing course for about 15 minutes.

Lesson 120

Materials Needed
- SCM science course of choice
- Math course of choice

Science: In your SCM science course, complete the second assignment for Week 24.

Math: Work on your selected math curriculum for about 30 minutes.

Tip: Remind your student to record in his Book of Mottoes any meaningful quotations, poetry, excerpts, or Scripture passages from recent readings (if he is interested in that ongoing project).

Term 3

(12 weeks; 5 lessons/week)

Term 3 Resources List

- *Spelling Wisdom, Book 2*
- *Using Language Well, Book 2, Student Book*
- *Using Language Well, Book 2, Teacher Guide and Answer Key*
- Simply Charlotte Mason (SCM) science course of choice
- *Journaling a Year in Nature* notebooks (optional)
- Typing course of choice
- Math course of choice

Weekly Schedule

Day One	Day Two	Day Three	Day Four	Day Five
Math (20–30 min.)	Math (20–30 min.)	Math (20–30 min.)	Math (20–30 min.)	Math (20–30 min.)
	Science (20–30 min.)		(Nature Study)	Science (20–30 min.)
Typing (10–15 min.)		Spelling Wisdom & Using Language Well (15–20 min.)	Typing (10–15 min.)	Spelling Wisdom & Using Language Well (15–20 min.)

Lesson 121

Materials Needed
- Math course of choice
- Typing course of choice

Math: Work on your selected math curriculum for about 30 minutes.

Typing: Work on your selected typing course for about 15 minutes.

Reminder: Assign your student to write one narration from his history, geography, Bible, or science readings this week. Use Rubric 2.3 from Using Language Well, Book 2, Teacher Guide and Answer Key *to help you evaluate his writing. Continue oral narrations daily.*

Lesson 122

Materials Needed
- SCM science course of choice
- Math course of choice

Science: In your SCM science course, complete the first assignment for Week 25.

Math: Work on your selected math curriculum for about 30 minutes.

Lesson 123

Materials Needed
- Math course of choice
- *Spelling Wisdom, Book 2*
- *Using Language Well, Book 2, Student Book*
- *Using Language Well, Book 2, Teacher Guide and Answer Key*

Math: Work on your selected math curriculum for about 30 minutes.

Spelling and Grammar: Complete *Using Language Well, Book 2,* lesson 49.

Lesson 124

Materials Needed
- Typing course of choice
- Math course of choice
- *Journaling a Year in Nature* notebooks (optional)

Typing: Work on your selected typing course for about 15 minutes.

Notes

Math: Work on your selected math curriculum for about 30 minutes.

Nature Study: Take the whole family outside for nature study.

Lesson 125

Materials Needed
- SCM science course of choice
- Math course of choice
- *Spelling Wisdom, Book 2*
- *Using Language Well, Book 2, Student Book*
- *Using Language Well, Book 2, Teacher Guide and Answer Key*

Science: In your SCM science course, complete the second assignment for Week 25.

Math: Work on your selected math curriculum for about 30 minutes.

Spelling and Grammar: Complete *Using Language Well, Book 2,* lesson 50.

Lesson 126

Materials Needed
- Math course of choice
- Typing course of choice

Math: Work on your selected math curriculum for about 30 minutes.

Typing: Work on your selected typing course for about 15 minutes.

Reminder: Assign your student to write one narration from his history, geography, Bible, or science readings this week. Use Rubric 2.3 from Using Language Well, Book 2, Teacher Guide and Answer Key *to help you evaluate his writing. Continue oral narrations daily.*

Lesson 127

Materials Needed
- SCM science course of choice
- Math course of choice

Science: In your SCM science course, complete the first assignment for Week 26.

Math: Work on your selected math curriculum for about 30 minutes.

Lesson 128

Materials Needed
- Math course of choice
- *Spelling Wisdom, Book 2*
- *Using Language Well, Book 2, Student Book*
- *Using Language Well, Book 2, Teacher Guide and Answer Key*

Math: Work on your selected math curriculum for about 30 minutes.

Spelling and Grammar: Complete *Using Language Well, Book 2,* lesson 51.

Lesson 129

Materials Needed
- Typing course of choice
- Math course of choice
- *Journaling a Year in Nature* notebooks (optional)

Typing: Work on your selected typing course for about 15 minutes.

Math: Work on your selected math curriculum for about 30 minutes.

Nature Study: Take the whole family outside for nature study.

Lesson 130

Materials Needed
- SCM science course of choice
- Math course of choice
- *Spelling Wisdom, Book 2*
- *Using Language Well, Book 2, Student Book*
- *Using Language Well, Book 2, Teacher Guide and Answer Key*

Science: In your SCM science course, complete the second assignment for Week 26.

Math: Work on your selected math curriculum for about 30 minutes.

Spelling and Grammar: Complete *Using Language Well, Book 2,* lesson 52.

Lesson 131

Materials Needed
- Math course of choice
- Typing course of choice

Math: Work on your selected math curriculum for about 30 minutes.

Typing: Work on your selected typing course for about 15 minutes.

Reminder: Assign your student to write one narration from his history, geography, Bible, or science readings this week. Use Rubric 2.3 from Using Language Well, Book 2, Teacher Guide and Answer Key *to help you evaluate his writing. Continue oral narrations daily.*

Lesson 132

Materials Needed
- SCM science course of choice
- Math course of choice

Science: In your SCM science course, complete the first assignment for Week 27.

Math: Work on your selected math curriculum for about 30 minutes.

Tip: Remind your student to record in his Book of Mottoes any meaningful quotations, poetry, excerpts, or Scripture passages from recent readings (if he is interested in that ongoing project).

Lesson 133

Materials Needed
- Math course of choice
- *Spelling Wisdom, Book 2*
- *Using Language Well, Book 2, Student Book*
- *Using Language Well, Book 2, Teacher Guide and Answer Key*

Math: Work on your selected math curriculum for about 30 minutes.

Spelling and Grammar: Complete *Using Language Well, Book 2,* lesson 53.

Lesson 134

Materials Needed
- Typing course of choice
- Math course of choice
- *Journaling a Year in Nature* notebooks (optional)

Typing: Work on your selected typing course for about 15 minutes.

Math: Work on your selected math curriculum for about 30 minutes.

Nature Study: Take the whole family outside for nature study.

Lesson 135

Materials Needed
- SCM science course of choice
- Math course of choice
- *Spelling Wisdom, Book 2*
- *Using Language Well, Book 2, Student Book*
- *Using Language Well, Book 2, Teacher Guide and Answer Key*

Science: In your SCM science course, complete the second assignment for Week 27.

Math: Work on your selected math curriculum for about 30 minutes.

Spelling and Grammar: Complete *Using Language Well, Book 2,* lesson 54.

Lesson 136

Materials Needed
- Math course of choice
- Typing course of choice

Math: Work on your selected math curriculum for about 30 minutes.

Typing: Work on your selected typing course for about 15 minutes.

Reminder: Assign your student to write one narration from his history, geography, Bible, or science readings this week. Use Rubric 2.3 from Using Language Well, Book 2, Teacher Guide and Answer Key *to help you evaluate his writing. Continue oral narrations daily.*

Lesson 137

Materials Needed
- SCM science course of choice
- Math course of choice

Science: In your SCM science course, complete the first assignment for Week 28.

Math: Work on your selected math curriculum for about 30 minutes.

Lesson 138

Materials Needed
- Math course of choice
- *Spelling Wisdom, Book 2*
- *Using Language Well, Book 2, Student Book*
- *Using Language Well, Book 2, Teacher Guide and Answer Key*

Math: Work on your selected math curriculum for about 30 minutes.

Spelling and Grammar: Complete *Using Language Well, Book 2*, lesson 55.

Lesson 139

Materials Needed
- Typing course of choice
- Math course of choice
- *Journaling a Year in Nature* notebooks (optional)

Typing: Work on your selected typing course for about 15 minutes.

Math: Work on your selected math curriculum for about 30 minutes.

Nature Study: Take the whole family outside for nature study.

Lesson 140

Materials Needed
- SCM science course of choice
- Math course of choice
- *Spelling Wisdom, Book 2*
- *Using Language Well, Book 2, Student Book*
- *Using Language Well, Book 2, Teacher Guide and Answer Key*

Science: In your SCM science course, complete the second assignment for Week 28.

Math: Work on your selected math curriculum for about 30 minutes.

Spelling and Grammar: Complete *Using Language Well, Book 2*, lesson 56.

Lesson 141

Materials Needed
- Math course of choice
- Typing course of choice

Math: Work on your selected math curriculum for about 30 minutes.

Typing: Work on your selected typing course for about 15 minutes.

Reminder: Assign your student to write one narration from his history, geography, Bible, or science readings this week. Use Rubric 2.3 from Using Language Well, Book 2, Teacher Guide and Answer Key *to help you evaluate his writing. Continue oral narrations daily.*

Lesson 142

Materials Needed
- SCM science course of choice
- Math course of choice

Science: In your SCM science course, complete the first assignment for Week 29.

Math: Work on your selected math curriculum for about 30 minutes.

Lesson 143

Materials Needed
- Math course of choice
- *Spelling Wisdom, Book 2*
- *Using Language Well, Book 2, Student Book*
- *Using Language Well, Book 2, Teacher Guide and Answer Key*

Math: Work on your selected math curriculum for about 30 minutes.

Spelling and Grammar: Complete *Using Language Well, Book 2,* lesson 57.

Lesson 144

Materials Needed
- Typing course of choice
- Math course of choice
- *Journaling a Year in Nature* notebooks (optional)

Typing: Work on your selected typing course for about 15 minutes.

Math: Work on your selected math curriculum for about 30 minutes.

Nature Study: Take the whole family outside for nature study.

Lesson 145

Materials Needed
- SCM science course of choice

- Math course of choice
- *Spelling Wisdom, Book 2*
- *Using Language Well, Book 2, Student Book*
- *Using Language Well, Book 2, Teacher Guide and Answer Key*

Science: In your SCM science course, complete the second assignment for Week 29.

Math: Work on your selected math curriculum for about 30 minutes.

Spelling and Grammar: Complete *Using Language Well, Book 2,* lesson 58.

Lesson 146

Materials Needed
- Math course of choice
- Typing course of choice

Math: Work on your selected math curriculum for about 30 minutes.

Typing: Work on your selected typing course for about 15 minutes.

Reminder: Assign your student to write one narration from his history, geography, Bible, or science readings this week. Use Rubric 2.3 from Using Language Well, Book 2, Teacher Guide and Answer Key *to help you evaluate his writing. Continue oral narrations daily.*

Lesson 147

Materials Needed
- SCM science course of choice
- Math course of choice

Science: In your SCM science course, complete the first assignment for Week 30.

Math: Work on your selected math curriculum for about 30 minutes.

Tip: Remind your student to record in his Book of Mottoes any meaningful quotations, poetry, excerpts, or Scripture passages from recent readings (if he is interested in that ongoing project).

Lesson 148

Materials Needed
- Math course of choice

- *Spelling Wisdom, Book 2*
- *Using Language Well, Book 2, Student Book*
- *Using Language Well, Book 2, Teacher Guide and Answer Key*

Math: Work on your selected math curriculum for about 30 minutes.

Spelling and Grammar: Complete *Using Language Well, Book 2,* lesson 59.

Lesson 149

Materials Needed
- Typing course of choice
- Math course of choice
- *Journaling a Year in Nature* notebooks (optional)

Typing: Work on your selected typing course for about 15 minutes.

Math: Work on your selected math curriculum for about 30 minutes.

Nature Study: Take the whole family outside for nature study.

Lesson 150

Materials Needed
- SCM science course of choice
- Math course of choice
- *Spelling Wisdom, Book 2*
- *Using Language Well, Book 2, Student Book*
- *Using Language Well, Book 2, Teacher Guide and Answer Key*

Science: In your SCM science course, complete the second assignment for Week 30.

Math: Work on your selected math curriculum for about 30 minutes.

Spelling and Grammar: Complete *Using Language Well, Book 2,* lesson 60.

Lesson 151

Materials Needed
- Math course of choice
- Typing course of choice

Math: Work on your selected math curriculum for about 30 minutes.

Typing: Work on your selected typing course for about 15 minutes.

Reminder: Assign your student to write one narration from his history, geography, Bible, or science readings this week. Use Rubric 2.3 from Using Language Well, Book 2, Teacher Guide and Answer Key *to help you evaluate his writing. Continue oral narrations daily.*

Lesson 152

Materials Needed
- SCM science course of choice
- Math course of choice

Science: In your SCM science course, complete the first assignment for Week 31.

Math: Work on your selected math curriculum for about 30 minutes.

Lesson 153

Materials Needed
- Math course of choice
- *Spelling Wisdom, Book 2*
- *Using Language Well, Book 2, Student Book*
- *Using Language Well, Book 2, Teacher Guide and Answer Key*

Math: Work on your selected math curriculum for about 30 minutes.

Spelling and Grammar: Complete *Using Language Well, Book 2,* lesson 61.

Lesson 154

Materials Needed
- Typing course of choice
- Math course of choice
- *Journaling a Year in Nature* notebooks (optional)

Typing: Work on your selected typing course for about 15 minutes.

Math: Work on your selected math curriculum for about 30 minutes.

Nature Study: Take the whole family outside for nature study.

Lesson 155

Materials Needed
- SCM science course of choice
- Math course of choice
- *Spelling Wisdom, Book 2*

- *Using Language Well, Book 2, Student Book*
- *Using Language Well, Book 2, Teacher Guide and Answer Key*

Science: In your SCM science course, complete the second assignment for Week 31.

Math: Work on your selected math curriculum for about 30 minutes.

Spelling and Grammar: Complete *Using Language Well, Book 2,* lesson 62.

Lesson 156

Materials Needed
- Math course of choice
- Typing course of choice

Math: Work on your selected math curriculum for about 30 minutes.

Typing: Work on your selected typing course for about 15 minutes.

Reminder: Assign your student to write one narration from his history, geography, Bible, or science readings this week. Use Rubric 2.3 from Using Language Well, Book 2, Teacher Guide and Answer Key *to help you evaluate his writing. Continue oral narrations daily.*

Lesson 157

Materials Needed
- SCM science course of choice
- Math course of choice

Science: In your SCM science course, complete the first assignment for Week 32.

Math: Work on your selected math curriculum for about 30 minutes.

Lesson 158

Materials Needed
- Math course of choice
- *Spelling Wisdom, Book 2*
- *Using Language Well, Book 2, Student Book*
- *Using Language Well, Book 2, Teacher Guide and Answer Key*

Math: Work on your selected math curriculum for about 30 minutes.

Spelling and Grammar: Complete *Using Language Well, Book 2,* lesson 63.

Lesson 159

Materials Needed
- Typing course of choice
- Math course of choice
- *Journaling a Year in Nature* notebooks (optional)

Typing: Work on your selected typing course for about 15 minutes.

Math: Work on your selected math curriculum for about 30 minutes.

Nature Study: Take the whole family outside for nature study.

Lesson 160

Materials Needed
- SCM science course of choice
- Math course of choice
- *Spelling Wisdom, Book 2*
- *Using Language Well, Book 2, Student Book*
- *Using Language Well, Book 2, Teacher Guide and Answer Key*

Science: In your SCM science course, complete the second assignment for Week 32.

Math: Work on your selected math curriculum for about 30 minutes.

Spelling and Grammar: Complete *Using Language Well, Book 2,* lesson 64.

Lesson 161

Materials Needed
- Math course of choice
- Typing course of choice

Math: Work on your selected math curriculum for about 30 minutes.

Typing: Work on your selected typing course for about 15 minutes.

Reminder: Assign your student to write one narration from his history, geography, Bible, or science readings this week. Use Rubric 2.3 from Using Language Well, Book 2, Teacher Guide and Answer Key *to help you evaluate his writing. Continue oral narrations daily.*

Lesson 162

Materials Needed
- SCM science course of choice
- Math course of choice

Science: In your SCM science course, complete the first assignment for Week 33.

Math: Work on your selected math curriculum for about 30 minutes.

Tip: Remind your student to record in his Book of Mottoes any meaningful quotations, poetry, excerpts, or Scripture passages from recent readings (if he is interested in that ongoing project).

Lesson 163

Materials Needed
- Math course of choice
- *Spelling Wisdom, Book 2*
- *Using Language Well, Book 2, Student Book*
- *Using Language Well, Book 2, Teacher Guide and Answer Key*

Math: Work on your selected math curriculum for about 30 minutes.

Spelling and Grammar: Complete *Using Language Well, Book 2,* lesson 65.

Lesson 164

Materials Needed
- Typing course of choice
- Math course of choice
- *Journaling a Year in Nature* notebooks (optional)

Typing: Work on your selected typing course for about 15 minutes.

Math: Work on your selected math curriculum for about 30 minutes.

Nature Study: Take the whole family outside for nature study.

Lesson 165

Materials Needed
- SCM science course of choice
- Math course of choice
- *Spelling Wisdom, Book 2*

- *Using Language Well, Book 2, Student Book*
- *Using Language Well, Book 2, Teacher Guide and Answer Key*

Science: In your SCM science course, complete the second assignment for Week 33.

Math: Work on your selected math curriculum for about 30 minutes.

Spelling and Grammar: Complete *Using Language Well, Book 2,* lesson 66.

Lesson 166

Materials Needed
- Math course of choice
- Typing course of choice

Math: Work on your selected math curriculum for about 30 minutes.

Typing: Work on your selected typing course for about 15 minutes.

Reminder: Assign your student to write one narration from his history, geography, Bible, or science readings this week. Use Rubric 2.3 from Using Language Well, Book 2, Teacher Guide and Answer Key *to help you evaluate his writing. Continue oral narrations daily.*

Lesson 167

Materials Needed
- SCM science course of choice
- Math course of choice

Science: In your SCM science course, complete the first assignment for Week 34.

Math: Work on your selected math curriculum for about 30 minutes.

Lesson 168

Materials Needed
- Math course of choice
- *Spelling Wisdom, Book 2*
- *Using Language Well, Book 2, Student Book*
- *Using Language Well, Book 2, Teacher Guide and Answer Key*

Math: Work on your selected math curriculum for about 30 minutes.

Spelling and Grammar: Complete *Using Language Well, Book 2,* lesson 67.

Lesson 169

Materials Needed
- Typing course of choice
- Math course of choice
- *Journaling a Year in Nature* notebooks (optional)

Typing: Work on your selected typing course for about 15 minutes.

Math: Work on your selected math curriculum for about 30 minutes.

Nature Study: Take the whole family outside for nature study.

Lesson 170

Materials Needed
- SCM science course of choice
- Math course of choice
- *Spelling Wisdom, Book 2*
- *Using Language Well, Book 2, Student Book*
- *Using Language Well, Book 2, Teacher Guide and Answer Key*

Science: In your SCM science course, complete the second assignment for Week 34.

Math: Work on your selected math curriculum for about 30 minutes.

Spelling and Grammar: Complete *Using Language Well, Book 2*, lesson 68.

Lesson 171

Materials Needed
- Math course of choice
- Typing course of choice

Math: Work on your selected math curriculum for about 30 minutes.

Typing: Work on your selected typing course for about 15 minutes.

Reminder: Assign your student to write one narration from his history, geography, Bible, or science readings this week. Use Rubric 2.3 from Using Language Well, Book 2, Teacher Guide and Answer Key *to help you evaluate his writing. Continue oral narrations daily.*

Lesson 172

Materials Needed
- SCM science course of choice
- Math course of choice

Science: In your SCM science course, complete the first assignment for Week 35.

Math: Work on your selected math curriculum for about 30 minutes.

Lesson 173

Materials Needed
- Math course of choice
- *Spelling Wisdom, Book 2*
- *Using Language Well, Book 2, Student Book*
- *Using Language Well, Book 2, Teacher Guide and Answer Key*

Math: Work on your selected math curriculum for about 30 minutes.

Spelling and Grammar: Complete *Using Language Well, Book 2,* lesson 69.

Lesson 174

Materials Needed
- Typing course of choice
- Math course of choice
- *Journaling a Year in Nature* notebooks (optional)

Typing: Work on your selected typing course for about 15 minutes.

Math: Work on your selected math curriculum for about 30 minutes.

Nature Study: Take the whole family outside for nature study.

Lesson 175

Materials Needed
- SCM science course of choice
- Math course of choice
- *Spelling Wisdom, Book 2*
- *Using Language Well, Book 2, Student Book*
- *Using Language Well, Book 2, Teacher Guide and Answer Key*

Science: In your SCM science course, complete the second assignment for Week 35.

Math: Work on your selected math curriculum for about 30 minutes.

Spelling and Grammar: Complete *Using Language Well, Book 2,* lesson 70.

Lesson 176

Materials Needed
- Math course of choice
- Typing course of choice

Math: Work on your selected math curriculum for about 30 minutes.

Typing: Work on your selected typing course for about 15 minutes.

Reminder: Assign your student to write one narration from his history, geography, Bible, or science readings this week. Use Rubric 2.3 from Using Language Well, Book 2, Teacher Guide and Answer Key *to help you evaluate his writing. Continue oral narrations daily.*

Lesson 177

Materials Needed
- SCM science course of choice
- Math course of choice

Science: In your SCM science course, complete the first assignment for Week 36.

Math: Work on your selected math curriculum for about 30 minutes.

Tip: Remind your student to record in his Book of Mottoes any meaningful quotations, poetry, excerpts, or Scripture passages from recent readings (if he is interested in that ongoing project).

Lesson 178

Materials Needed
- Math course of choice
- *Spelling Wisdom, Book 2*
- *Using Language Well, Book 2, Student Book*
- *Using Language Well, Book 2, Teacher Guide and Answer Key*

Math: Work on your selected math curriculum for about 30 minutes.

Spelling and Grammar: Use today and lesson 180 to catch up on any assignments in *Using Language Well, Book 2,* as needed.

Lesson 179

Materials Needed
- Typing course of choice
- Math course of choice
- *Journaling a Year in Nature* notebooks (optional)

Typing: Work on your selected typing course for about 15 minutes.

Math: Work on your selected math curriculum for about 30 minutes.

Nature Study: Take the whole family outside for nature study.

Lesson 180

Materials Needed
- SCM science course of choice
- Math course of choice
- *Spelling Wisdom, Book 2*
- *Using Language Well, Book 2, Student Book*
- *Using Language Well, Book 2, Teacher Guide and Answer Key*

Science: In your SCM science course, complete the second assignment for Week 36.

Math: Work on your selected math curriculum for about 30 minutes.

Spelling and Grammar: Use today to catch up on any assignments in *Using Language Well, Book 2,* as needed.